CREATE A PATH THAT REFLECTS WHO YOU ARE.

ALSO BY MEERA LEE PATEL

*How It Feels to Find Yourself: Navigating Life's
Changes with Purpose, Clarity, and Heart*

My Friend Fear: Finding Magic in the Unknown

JOURNALS

Create Your Own Calm: A Journal for Quieting Anxiety

Made Out of Stars: A Journal for Self-Realization

Start Where You Are: A Journal for Self-Exploration

go your own way

MEERA LEE PATEL

Bestselling author of START WHERE YOU ARE

A TarcherPerigee Book

tarcherperigee

an imprint of Penguin Random House LLC
penguinrandomhouse.com

Copyright © 2023 by Meera Lee Patel
Penguin Random House supports copyright. Copyright fuels creativity,
encourages diverse voices, promotes free speech, and creates a vibrant culture.
Thank you for buying an authorized edition of this book and for complying with
copyright laws by not reproducing, scanning, or distributing any part of it in
any form without permission. You are supporting writers and allowing Penguin
Random House to continue to publish books for every reader.

TarcherPerigee with tp colophon is a registered trademark of Penguin Random
House LLC.

Most TarcherPerigee books are available at special quantity discounts for bulk
purchase for sales promotions, premiums, fund-raising, and educational needs.
Special books or book excerpts also can be created to fit specific needs. For details,
write SpecialMarkets@penguinrandomhouse.com.

ISBN: 9780593418758

Printed in China
1   3   5   7   9   10   8   6   4   2

Book design by Meera Lee Patel

To you, for summoning the courage
and the confidence to go your own way

I USED to THINK I
WAS THE STRANGEST
PERSON IN THE WORLD
BUT THEN I THOUGHT
THERE ARE SO MANY
PEOPLE IN THE WORLD,
THERE MUST BE SOMEONE
JUST LIKE ME WHO FEELS
BIZARRE AND FLAWED
IN THE SAME WAYS I
DO. I WOULD IMAGINE
HER, AND IMAGINE
THAT SHE MUST BE
OUT THERE THINKING
OF ME, TOO. WELL, I
HOPE THAT IF YOU ARE
OUT THERE AND READ
THIS AND KNOW THAT,
YES, IT'S TRUE I'M HERE,
AND I'M JUST AS
STRANGE AS YOU.

FRIDA KAHLO

INTRODUCTION

I wasn't raised to be confident.

I was a stubborn child, which worried my family. Stubbornness was perceived as a detriment, a pestering characteristic that would almost certainly repel potential relationships and opportunities. As a young girl raised by immigrant parents, I was taught to be accommodating, modest, and grateful for all I had. It wasn't until I was a fully grown adult that I began to appreciate my stubbornness for what it really was: a sign of my dedication, persistence, and belief in myself.

It's nearly impossible to possess self-confidence when you feel like an outsider. Growing up as one of few BIPOC families in a wealthy, all-white town meant that besides my family, there was no one who looked like me. There was no one who also struggled to straddle two worlds, no one who could relate to what it feels like to be a third-culture kid. This inability to relate to any of my peers during my developmental years—for my entire adolescence—led me to despise anything that made me different from the people around me. It made me despise myself.

I spent years lightening my skin, hanging my hopes of acceptance on bleach creams and scrubs. I thought if I scrubbed hard enough, my brown skin would eventually give way to white. I stopped speaking my native language, opting only for English, especially around classmates and friends. I stopped being myself because what I wanted more than anything else was to be accepted—and to me, that meant being someone else.

The hardest part about childhood is that you have little choice about where you live and the people, environment, and culture that's accessible to you. You believe that the small world around you is indicative of the entire world. It's difficult to comprehend that another world, another life—can exist.

As I grew older my environment changed, and the world—or what I knew of it—split wide open. I attended a performing arts high school that prioritized diversity. I was no longer restricted to the presence of the few dozen peers I grew up with. Instead, I met intelligent and creative students from all over the state. I met people from a range of economic backgrounds, ethnicities, languages, family dynamics, and interests. Everyone was different, and all the more beautiful because of it. This was the first time in my young life that I clearly remember feeling less alone. I felt proud of what set me apart from everyone else, and my confidence bloomed.

Throughout the years, I've realized that my differences are strengths. This includes my skin color, my culture, and my language, but extends to include my thoughts, my philosophies, my beliefs, and my values—and how I choose to practice them. These elements come together to form the essence of who I am. In moments of doubt and insecurity, I remind myself that no other person can think like me, nurture friendships like me, express themselves like me, create as I do. My voice is who I am, and the person I am uniquely connects me to the world.

When facing your own moments of doubt or insecurity, I want you to remind yourself of the very same: Your voice is who you are and the person you are uniquely connects you to the world. You have the ability to leave an impression on each person you meet and the part of their life you touch. Use this reminder to instill confidence and love within yourself.

Self-confidence is knowing yourself deeply; accepting yourself and your imperfections; and loving yourself through impatience, mistake-making, and life's messiness. Approach yourself the way you would a loved one—with the same understanding, love, and forgiveness—and with the same kind heart. Confidence isn't floating through life with perfect poise and grace. Confidence is understanding that you will inevitably make mistakes but trusting in your ability to change course and, if necessary, begin again. Confidence is the acceptance and owning of your own power—the power to adapt, change, and rise to the challenges in front of you. Confidence is having the strength and humility necessary for changing your mind.

How do you become more confident? Self-confidence grows when you stop trying to be anyone other than who you are—when you lean into the core of yourself with the intention to understand who you are even more deeply. Self-confidence grows when you take care of yourself—when you put healthy foods into your body, move your body in the ways that nourish it, and get enough sleep. Self-confidence grows when you talk to and look at yourself with love and kindness; eventually, you will believe that you are someone worthy of both.

Self-confidence grows when you practice something that doesn't come easily—from becoming comfortable with small talk to mastering a new skill or language. Remember that what looks like it came easily to others is often the result of practice and persistence, not innate ability. As you become familiar with this discomfort, you'll feel more confident in your ability to learn and navigate new experiences. Your entire world will open up. Things will feel more possible because they will be more possible.

Make decisions that reflect who you are, even if they don't carry the promise of acceptance or approval from others. Live according to the values that make sense to your heart and mind. Listen to your own ideas. Make yourself proud. Remember that you will stumble and fall, but that it's within you to stand up and try again—and that confidence, and comfort, will always find you when you go your own way.

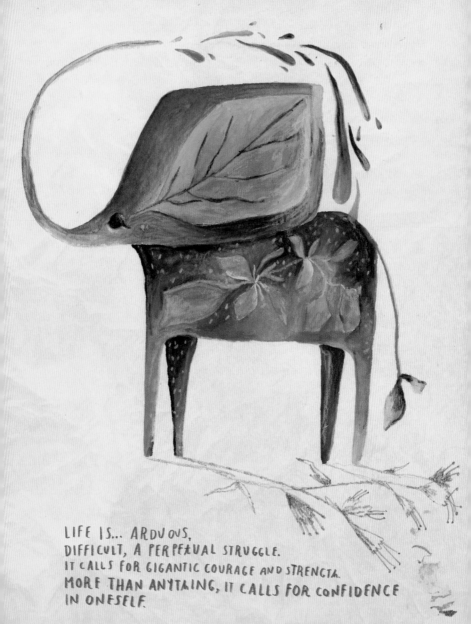

LIFE IS... ARDUOUS,
DIFFICULT, A PERPETUAL STRUGGLE.
IT CALLS FOR GIGANTIC COURAGE AND STRENGTH.
MORE THAN ANYTHING, IT CALLS FOR CONFIDENCE
IN ONESELF.

VIRGINIA WOOLF

Identify how much self-confidence you carry within:

On a scale of 1–10, how confident do you generally feel?

1   —   —   —   —   —   —   —   10
(I have trouble loving myself)   (I feel love for myself daily)

On a scale of 1–10, where do you feel the most confident?

IN MY BODY:

1   —   —   —   —   —   —   —   10
(I have trouble loving myself)   (I feel love for myself daily)

IN MY MIND:

1   —   —   —   —   —   —   —   10
(I have trouble loving myself)   (I feel love for myself daily)

IN MY HEART:

1   —   —   —   —   —   —   —   10
(I have trouble loving myself)   (I feel love for myself daily)

IN MY SPIRIT:

1   —   —   —   —   —   —   —   10
(I have trouble loving myself)   (I feel love for myself daily)

YOU GAIN STRENGTH, COURAGE, AND
CONFIDENCE BY EVERY EXPERIENCE
IN WHICH YOU REALLY STOP TO
LOOK *FEAR IN THE FACE.*
*you must do the thing you
think you cannot do.*

ELEANOR ROOSEVELT

What is something that feels out of reach?

Why does it feel impossible?

What would make it feel more possible?

I crossed the street to walk in the sunshine.

ELIZABETH GILBERT

Write down 3 thoughts that routinely bring you to a place of self-doubt. Now replace each one with a thought that brings you hope and the excitement of possibility.

Doubtful thought:

Motivating thought:

Doubtful thought:

Motivating thought:

Doubtful thought:

Motivating thought:

Remember that although many things are outside of our control, our thoughts are not—and reframing them gives us the confidence to act.

LET YOUR OWN UNIVERSE GUIDE YOU.

*Identifying your strengths helps you exercise them
in moments of doubt and insecurity.*

1. A strength I have is:

   a. A situation where this strength was helpful:

   b. A future scenario where it can be helpful:

2. A strength I have is:

   a. A situation where this strength was helpful:

   b. A future scenario where it can be helpful:

3. A strength I have is:

   a. A situation where this strength was helpful:

   b. A future scenario where it can be helpful:

4. A strength I have is:

   a. A situation where this strength was helpful:

   b. A future scenario where it can be helpful:

[SELF-RESPECT]...COMES TO US WHEN
WE ARE ALONE, IN QUIET MOMENTS, IN
QUIET PLACES, WHEN WE SUDDENLY
REALIZE THAT, KNOWING THE GOOD,
WE HAVE DONE IT; KNOWING THE
BEAUTIFUL, WE HAVE SERVED IT;
KNOWING THE TRUTH, WE HAVE
SPOKEN IT.

ALFRED WHITNEY GRISWOLD

A time I did what was right, though no one saw:

A time I found beauty in a challenging situation:

A time I spoke honestly, despite how difficult it was:

THE HUMAN SPIRIT IS TREMENDOUSLY RESILIENT.

— SHEILA WILLIAMS

Create a positive affirmation you can repeat to yourself in moments of doubt. Write it below in large letters. Tear this page out and pin it somewhere you'll see it daily.

Nothing and nobody is obliged to save you but you.

TONI MORRISON

Recognizing that you can help yourself is empowering.
List 5 positive changes you can create in your life:

1. I can

2. I can

3. I can

4. I can

5. I can

IF YOU BEGIN TO UNDERSTAND WHAT YOU ARE WITHOUT TRYING TO CHANGE IT, THEN WHAT YOU ARE UNDERGOES A TRANSFORMATION.

JIDDU KRISHNAMURTI

What I want most from myself:

How I want to feel toward myself:

What I want most from others:

How I want to feel toward them:

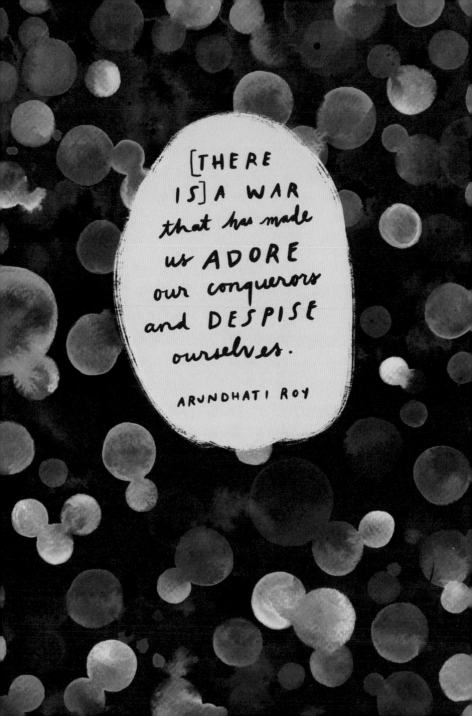

[THERE IS] A WAR that has made us ADORE our conquerors and DESPISE ourselves.

ARUNDHATI ROY

Who are the people that make you feel uncertain and insecure?

List them here:

A healthy relationship challenges you to become a better version of yourself; an unhealthy relationship asks you to change yourself into someone you aren't. Cross out the unhealthy relationships listed above.

1. The relationship I have with:

   a. Why it makes me feel insecure:

   b. Can this be a healthy relationship for me? Yes/No

2. The relationship I have with:

   a. Why it makes me feel insecure:

   b. Can this be a healthy relationship for me? Yes/No

3. The relationship I have with:

   a. Why it makes me feel insecure:

   b. Can this be a healthy relationship for me? Yes/No

THE WILLINGNESS to ACCEPT RESPONSIBILITY FOR ONE'S OWN LIFE...IS tHE SOURCE FROM WHICH SELF-RESPECT SPRINGS.

JOAN DIDION

Identify a current hardship where you are assigning blame externally. Accepting responsibility for the situation you're in allows you to regain control and act, which builds confidence in yourself and your abilities.

CURRENT HARDSHIP:

WHO/WHAT I'M BLAMING:

MY ROLE IN THIS SITUATION:

WHAT I CAN DO NEXT:

There is a path that
connects you to your heart,
your spirit, your sense of self;
you look within to find it.

Understanding your own needs allows you to meet them,
ensuring you feel healthy, confident, and in control.

What my spirit needs
to feel strong

my path

What I need to feel
most like myself

What my heart needs
to feel steady

IF YOU WANT TO BE RESPECTED BY OTHERS, THE GREAT THING IS TO RESPECT YOURSELF.

FYODOR DOSTOYEVSKY

Respecting yourself often means setting boundaries
between what you are and aren't willing to do
(or who you are and aren't willing to be).

Think about a time where you felt taken advantage of.

What would you do differently this time?

A man with outward courage dares to die;
A man with inner courage dares to LIVE.

LAO TZU

If you were not afraid, what are 10 things you would do?

1.

2.

3.

4.

5.

6.

7.

8.

9.

10.

GO YOUR
OWN
WAY.

Forging a new path isn't always easy but it's often necessary. Take a large sheet of paper and draw, paint, or build your own navigational map, pinpointing the milestones below.

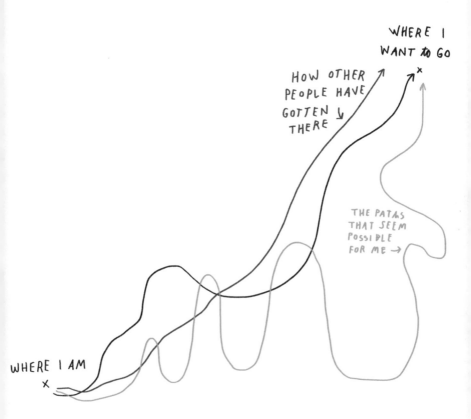

WHERE I WANT TO GO
x

HOW OTHER PEOPLE HAVE GOTTEN THERE

THE PATHS THAT SEEM POSSIBLE FOR ME →

WHERE I AM
x

You may not control all the events that happen to you, but you can decide not to be reduced by them. MAYA ANGELOU

Everything we survive deserves a celebration.
Identify 3 hardships you've endured, what you've learned
from them, and how they've strengthened you.

1. Moment of hardship:

    a. What I learned:

    b. How it strengthened me:

2. Moment of hardship:

    a. What I learned:

    b. How it strengthened me:

3. Moment of hardship:

    a. What I learned:

    b. How it strengthened me:

Remember that Wherever your heart is, there you will find your treasure.

PAULO COELHO

What do you value most in the world?

It's good to do uncomfortable things. It's weight training for life.

ANNE LAMOTT

If I knew this dream would come true, I would change:

1. My daily schedule in these ways:

2. The way I speak to myself:

3. The goals I set for myself:

THE SCARIEST
MOMENT IS ALWAYS
JUST BEFORE
YOU START.

STEPHEN KING

What is something that felt scary before you did it?

How did it feel after you began?

What lesson did you learn from the experience?

Shame corrodes
the very part of us
that believes we can
change and do better.

BRENÉ BROWN

It's often easier for us to be compassionate toward our friends and family than toward ourselves.

This exercise helps you treat yourself with the same love and compassion you give others.

Something I feel ashamed of:

If a friend shared this same feeling of shame with you, how would you respond to them? Write about it here:

NOT
KNOWING
WHEN THE DAWN
WILL COME, I
OPEN EVERY
DOOR.

EMILY
DICKINSON

Preparing for potential opportunities reduces
the amount of uncertainty we feel. It is a
building block for confidence.

1. If I didn't worry about what others thought, I would:

   I can work toward this by:

   One way I'll be ready for it when it arrives:

2. If I felt more confident in myself, I would:

   I can work toward this by:

   One way I'll be ready for it when it arrives:

3. If I wasn't worried about the consequence, I would:

   I can work toward this by:

   One way I'll be ready for it when it arrives:

To love
oneself is
the beginning
of a lifelong
romance.

OSCAR WILDE

How can I love myself more?

1. An action I can take to show myself love:

2. Words I can say to show myself love:

3. A gift I can give myself as an act of self-love:

4. How I can spend time to show myself love:

5. Something I can ask for to show myself love:

TO BE NOBODY-BUT-YOURSELF IN A
WORLD WHICH IS DOING ITS BEST, NIGHT AND
DAY, TO MAKE YOU EVERYBODY ELSE—
MEANS TO FIGHT THE HARDEST
BATTLE ANY HUMAN CAN FIGHT;

AND NEVER
STOP FIGHTING.

E.E. CUMMINGS

From the list below, circle 3 traits that are difficult to accept about yourself. Consider the idea that although these characteristics are challenging to navigate, they are also some of your greatest assets. How does each one uniquely contribute to who you are?

Anxious

Angry

Compassionate

Generous

Stubborn

Dedicated

Loyal

Strong

People-pleasing

Fickle

Smart

Agile

Indifferent

Thoughtful

Opinionated

Confident

Insecure

Helpful

Needy

Depressed

Self-critical

Challenging

Honest

Joyful

Hopeful

Realistic

Pessimistic

Encouraging

Critically-thinking

Nurturing

you are your
possibilities.

If you know
that, you can do
ANYTHING. OPRAH
WINFREY

Our brains protect us from failing by scaring us from starting. Identify 3 messages your inner critic tells you and consider how you can reframe these thoughts into helpful mantras.

My inner critic says, "You are...":

How it's trying to protect me:

How I can reframe these thoughts:

My inner critic says, "You are...":

How it's trying to protect me:

How I can reframe these thoughts:

My inner critic says, "You are...":

How it's trying to protect me:

How I can reframe these thoughts:

The greatest thing in the world is to know how to belong to oneself.

MICHEL DE MONTAIGNE

When do you feel most connected to yourself?

WHEN ONE IS PRETENDING, THE ENTIRE BODY REVOLTS.

ANAÏS NIN

I feel:

But I pretend that:

Instead, I'll:

I think:

But I pretend that:

Instead, I'll:

I want:

But I pretend that:

Instead, I'll:

I need:

But I pretend that:

Instead, I'll:

I say:

But I pretend that:

Instead, I'll:

No matter how hard the world pushes against me, within me,

there's something stronger—something better, pushing right back.

UNKNOWN

What is one belief that, without fail,
continues to motivate you?

ALL
the
art of
living
lies in
a fine
mingling of
LETTING
GO and HOLDING ON.

HAVELOCK ELLIS

What is something you're afraid of losing?

Why are you afraid of losing it?

How can you support yourself if you do lose it?

IF PEOPLE AVOID YOU, YOU WILL HAVE MORE TIME TO MEDITATE AND DO FINE RESEARCH ON A CURE FOR WHATEVER TRULY AFFLICTS YOU. MAYA ANGELOU

Not everyone is the right friend, partner, confidante, or family member for you. Identify the unhealthy relationships in your life, and then decide whether these can be nurtured back to health or if you're a healthier, happier person without them.

A person who makes me feel alone:

A person who doesn't understand me, or try to:

A person who is unsupportive or envious:

A person who makes me feel uncomfortable:

A person who is not interested in knowing me:

you must
really begin to
harden yourself to
the idea of
being worth
looking at.

JANE AUSTEN

I am a worthy friend because:

I am a worthy family member because:

I am a worthy person because:

I am a worthy caregiver because:

I'M SAFE INSIDE THIS CONTAINER CALLED ME.

HARUKI MURAKAMI

How do you keep yourself safe?

Nothing is better for self-esteem than SURVIVAL.

MARTHA GELLHORN

Reflect back on 3 occasions where you persevered through an experience you didn't think you had the strength to.

1.

2.

3.

I HAVE GREAT FAITH IN FOOLS—

SELF-CONFIDENCE

MY FRIENDS WILL CALL IT.

EDGAR ALLAN POE

A power pose can mentally transport you into a more confident, assertive state, even when you feel insecure or vulnerable. Common power poses are standing up straight with your hands on your hips or with your arms outstretched in a "V" shape over your head.

Write about an insecurity you have:

Take a deep breath, stand up, and assume a power pose for 60 seconds. Then write about the same insecurity again, paying close attention to any differences in how you feel:

List a fear you've recently overcome:

Now list two more fears you'd like to confront.
How can you push past each?

1. My fear:

   a. What it's telling me:

   b. An action I can take to push past it:

2. My fear:

   a. What it's telling me:

   b. An action I can take to push past it:

OUR
ABILITY TO
GROW IS
DIRECTLY PROPORTIONAL
TO AN ABILITY TO
entertain the
UNCOMFORTABLE.

TWYLA THARP

The last time I felt uncomfortable was when:

At the time, I wished:

Now, when I look back on the experience, I feel:

I grew from this experience by:

Next time I am in a similar situation, I will:

Live the questions now. Perhaps then, someday far in the future, you will gradually, without even noticing it, live your way into the answer.

RAINER
MARIA
RILKE

Security is trusting in yourself—understanding that although you may not have the answers right now, the challenges you face will eventually lead you to them.

There is no timeline for finding the answers; all you have to do is keep going.

1. Take a deep breath that fills your stomach and exhale audibly through your mouth.

2. Say aloud, "I am not running out of time".

Repeat this meditation 5 times, slowly.

PEOPLE GENERALLY
SEE WHAT THEY
LOOK FOR
AND HEAR WHAT THEY
LISTEN FOR.

HARPER LEE

Building confidence sometimes requires us to pretend
seeing what we'd like to see until we genuinely do.
Practice reframing how your inner critic talks to you.

I wish I could change this about myself:

I'm grateful for this part of myself because:

I wish I could change this about my thoughts:

I'm grateful for these thoughts because:

I wish I could change this about my body:

I'm grateful for this part of my body because:

I wish I could change this about my friendships:

I'm grateful for these friendships because:

I wish I could change this about my life:

I'm grateful for this part of my life because:

WHEN YOU'RE
DIFFERENT,
SOMETIMES
YOU DON'T SEE
THE MILLIONS
OF PEOPLE WHO
ACCEPT YOU FOR WHAT
YOU ARE. ALL YOU
NOTICE IS THE
PERSON WHO
DOESN'T.

JODI PICOULT

List the people in your life who love you for who you are.

Remember that they are safe places for you when
you feel unwanted or less than.

1.

2.

3.

Mutual respect and support breeds confidence in our
relationships with others. Send a quick message
(email, text, call, a note!) to one person from this list,
letting them know what they mean to you.

I CAN'T CHANGE WHERE I COME FROM OR WHAT I'VE BEEN THROUGH, SO WHY SHOULD I BE ASHAMED OF WHAT MAKES ME, ME?

ANGIE THOMAS

Dear Self,

I feel ashamed of:

I feel ashamed of it because:

OPTIONAL: Choose a trusted person from your list of
safe people to share this letter with. Remember that you
are strong: Vulnerability can only live inside strength,
and by exposing a source of shame, you are
taking steps to dissolve it.

The thing is to FREE ONE'S SELF: to let it find its dimensions, NOT BE IMPEDED.

VIRGINIA WOOLF

What is something that makes you feel free?

How can you access this freedom more frequently?

THE TRUE COURAGE IS IN FACING DANGER WHEN YOU ARE AFRAID.

L. FRANK BAUM

Think about a time you felt afraid
but forged ahead anyway. Reflect on it now.

A time I felt afraid was:

I decided to keep going by:

When I look back on it now, I feel:

Don't be satisfied
with stories, how
things have gone
with others.

UNFOLD
YOUR
OWN
MYTH.

RUMI

Comparing yourself with others is a guaranteed way to lose confidence in yourself and your own path. Take pride in the obstacles you face, knowing they are making you wiser, resilient, and expanding your capabilities.

1. Someone I compare myself with frequently is:

2. When I do this, I feel:

3. Instead of comparing myself, I will spend my energy doing this:

To be humble
IS TO BE GROUNDED
in knowing who
you are. It implies
the responsibility to
BECOME WHAT YOU WERE
meant to become —
TO GROW, TO REACH, TO FULLY
BLOOM as high and
strong and grand
AS YOU WERE CREATED
TO.

GLENNON DOYLE

*What makes you feel grounded, secure, and
confident in who you are?*

A person:

A place:

A book:

A song:

An activity:

I WILL NOT HAVE MY LIFE NARROWED DOWN. I WILL NOT BOW DOWN TO SOMEBODY ELSE'S WHIM OR TO SOMEONE ELSE'S IGNORANCE.

BELL HOOKS

Think about a time when someone made you feel small.

Write about it here:

Now, identify someone you admire for their confidence.

How would they have responded to this situation?

I AM
STRONGER·
than I am
BROKEN.

ROXANE GAY

Reflect on a time you experienced hurt and helped
yourself heal. Then take a few minutes to meditate
on your strengths, listing them below:

I was hurt when:

I healed by:

This experience shows me that my strengths are:

1.

2.

3.

4.

5.

TRUE SECURITY LIES IN THE UNRESTRAINED EMBRACE of INSECURITY—

IN THE RECOGNITION THAT WE NEVER REALLY STAND ON SOLID GROUND, AND NEVER CAN.

OLIVER BURKEMAN

Flexibility—the ability to adapt to life's inevitable changes—is the foundation of self-confidence.

Think about a hard-won milestone you've reached.

Map out the inevitable obstacles you overcame along the way below.

Where I began:

An obstacle I ran into:

How I overcame it:

A detour I had to take:

The milestone I reached:

How long I thought it'd take:

How long it actually took:

IN the
MIDST of TEARS,
I FOUND,
THERE WAS,
WITHIN ME,
AN
INVINCIBLE
SMILE.

ALBERT CAMUS

Validation often rests in being in service of others. A foolproof way to awaken dormant sources of confidence is by volunteering your time, energy, or services to someone who will benefit from it.

HOW I CAN HELP...

Someone in my family:

Someone in my life:

Someone I don't know:

WHERE I CAN HELP...

Within my workplace/school:

Within my neighborhood:

Within my community:

DON'T SET
YOUR GOALS
BY WHAT OTHER
PEOPLE
DEEM
IMPORTANT.

JAACHYNMA N.E. AGU

Write down 5 of your core values, the ones
that shape your ideal life.

1.

2.

3.

4.

5.

Make a vision board for this future life on a separate
piece of paper or board—it can be as big or small as you
like. Collage or draw the activities you'd engage in,
the people you'd spend your time with, and
the feelings you'd cultivate.

PEOPLE TALK ABOUT CONFIDENCE
WITHOUT EVER BRINGING UP HARD
WORK. THAT'S A MISTAKE...
CONFIDENCE IS LIKE RESPECT:
YOU HAVE TO EARN IT.

MINDY KALING

Feeling more comfortable in your body—and in your body's ability to care for you—leads to increased mental and emotional confidence. Choose a physical activity you'd like to feel more confident in—it can be anything from walking to yoga. Fill out the timeline below with the actions you'll take to get there.

I'd like to feel more confident in my ability to:

My confidence in this area (on a scale of 1—10):

WEEK 1 / Each day this week, I will:

WEEK 2 / Each day this week, I will:

WEEK 3 / Each day this week, I will:

WEEK 4 / Each day this week, I will:

After a month of consistently working on this, my confidence has:

My confidence in this area (on a scale of 1—10):

IT IS IN BOOKS,
POEMS, PAINTINGS
WHICH OFTEN GIVE US
THE CONFIDENCE TO
TAKE SERIOUSLY
FEELINGS IN OURSELVES
THAT WE MIGHT
OTHERWISE NEVER
HAVE THOUGHT TO
ACKNOWLEDGE.

ALAIN DE BOTTON

Identify the piece of art (song, painting, poem...or person!)
that helps you feel comfortable with the following feelings.

_____

helps me understand that shame is
something everyone feels.

_____

helps me understand that I'm not
the only one who feels guilty sometimes.

_____

teaches me that insecurity
is nothing to be ashamed of.

_____

shows me that I am worthy
of love, beauty, and satisfaction.

IT WAS NEVER THE RIGHT TIME, OR IT WAS ALWAYS THE RIGHT TIME, DEPENDING ON HOW YOU LOOKED AT IT.

ANN PATCHETT

Think of a specific event or period in your life
that didn't go as planned.

I planned on things going this way:

Instead, this is what happened:

At the time, I thought this was the right thing to do:

Looking back on it now, the best part of
this experience was:

Kindness is the
light that dissolves
ALL WALLS
between souls,
families + nations.

YOGANANDA

Practicing kindness with others builds supportive, mutual connection. Practicing kindness with yourself builds confidence—by taking care of yourself and your needs, you build the resilience needed to face disappointments.

Write a letter to your past self. Show gratitude for who you are and how far you've come. Acknowledge past mistakes and then forgive yourself for them. Place the letter in a safe place, reading it when you need to remind yourself that you are loved.

Nothing ever goes away until it has taught us what we need to know.

PEMA CHÖDRÖN

Identify a pattern in your life that continues to occur.
What lesson is life trying to teach you?

PATTERN:

LESSON I'M BEING TAUGHT:

FRIENDSHIP WITH
ONESELF IS ALL-IMPORTANT,
BECAUSE
WITHOUT IT
ONE
CANNOT BE
FRIENDS WITH ANYONE ELSE
IN tHE WORLD. ELEANOR
ROOSEVELT

Explore your friendship with yourself
using the prompts below.

WHAT I DO

I take care of myself by:

I show myself love by:

I respect myself by:

When I am by myself, I feel:

WHAT I CAN DO

I'd like to show myself love by:

I can listen to myself more closely by:

I can be gentle with myself by:

I can respect myself by:

WHAT I HOPE FOR

How I want to feel about myself:

How I'd like to think about myself:

How I'd like to treat myself:

LIFE IS NOT EASY FOR ANY OF US. BUT WHAT OF THAT? WE MUST HAVE PERSEVERANCE AND, ABOVE ALL, CONFIDENCE IN OURSELVES. WE MUST BELIEVE WE ARE GIFTED FOR SOMETHING AND THAT THIS THING, AT WHATEVER COST, MUST BE ATTAINED.

MARIE CURIE

Allow your past adventures—all the things you never thought you'd do—to give you confidence for persevering through new challenges. Draw or write about:

A place I never thought I'd see:

A physical activity I never thought I'd do:

A meal I never thought I'd eat:

A person I never thought I'd be friends with:

A room I never imagined I'd sleep in:

An accomplishment I never thought I'd celebrate:

A feeling I never thought I'd have:

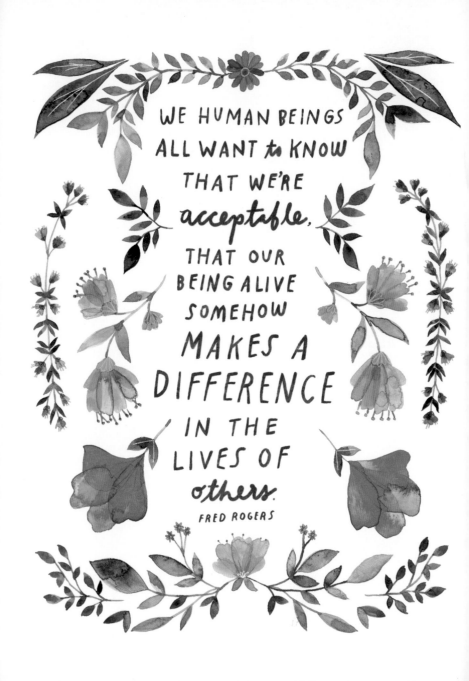

WE HUMAN BEINGS
ALL WANT to KNOW
THAT WE'RE
acceptable,
THAT OUR
BEING ALIVE
SOMEHOW
MAKES A
DIFFERENCE
IN THE
LIVES OF
others.
FRED ROGERS

List 3 things you've done that have made a difference
(however big or small!) in someone else's life.

1. Something I did:

   a. The difference it made:

2. Something I did:

   a. The difference it made:

3. Something I did:

   a. The difference it made:

WE BEGIN TO FIND
AND BECOME OURSELVES
WHEN WE NOTICE
HOW WE ARE
ALREADY FOUND,
ALREADY TRULY,
ENTIRELY, WILDLY,
MESSILY,
MARVELOUSLY
WHO WE WERE
BORN TO BE.

ANNE LAMOTT

List 5 ways that you are different from anyone else in the world. Think about the characteristics, thoughts, beliefs, values, and unique perspectives that separate you from everyone else—the essentials that make you who you are.

1.

2.

3.

4.

5.

BIBLIOGRAPHY

A Room of One's Own by Virginia Woolf (Mariner Books, 1989)

Ain't I a Woman: Black Women and Feminism by bell hooks (Routledge, 2014)

An Ideal Husband by Oscar Wilde (public domain)

Autobiography of a Yogi by Paramahansa Yogananda (Self-Realization Fellowship, 1998)

Bel Canto by Ann Patchett (Harper Perennial Modern Classics, 2008)

Believing in Ourselves by Armand Eisen (Ariel Books, 1992)

Change of Heart by Jodi Picoult (Atria Books, 2008)

Comfortable with Uncertainty by Pema Chödrön (Shambhala, 2003)

Coraline by Neil Gaiman (Bloomsbury, 2012)

Dictionary of Proverbs by G. Kleiser (APH Publishing, 2005)

E. E. Cummings: A Miscellany Revised by E. E. Cummings (October House, 1965)

Eat, Pray, Love by Elizabeth Gilbert (Penguin, 2006)

Egoists: A Book of Supermen by James Huneker (Scribner, 1909)

Griswold, Alfred Whitney. "Self-Respect Address." Yale University, 9 June 1957. New Haven, CT. Address.

Home by Toni Morrison (Alfred A. Knopf, 2012)

Hunger by Roxane Gay (Harper, 2017)

I Thought It Was Just Me (But It Isn't) by Brené Brown (Avery, 2007)

Kafka on the Shore by Haruki Murakami (Knopf Doubleday Publishing Group, 2006)

Letter to my Daughter by Maya Angelou (Random House, 2009)

Letters to a Young Poet by Rainer Maria Rilke (W. W. Norton & Company, 1993)

Made Out of Stars by Meera Lee Patel (TarcherPerigee, 2018)

Mansfield Park by Jane Austen (Penguin Books, 2003)

On Writing by Stephen King (Scribner, 2000)

Plan B by Anne Lamott (Riverhead Books, 2006)

Slouching Towards Bethlehem by Joan Didion (Farrar, Straus, and Giroux, 1968)

Tao Te Ching by Lao Tzu (Vintage, 1989)

The Alchemist by Paulo Coelho (HarperTorch, 1993)

The Antidote by Oliver Burkeman (Farrar, Straus, and Giroux, 2012)

The Architecture of Happiness by Alain De Botton (Vintage, 2008)

The Complete Essays by Michel de Montaigne (Penguin Classics, 1993)

The Complete Works of Edgar Allan Poe: Marginalia, Eureka by Edgar Allan Poe (Nabu Press, 2012)

The Creative Habit by Twyla Tharp (Simon & Schuster, 2006)

The Essential Rumi by Jalal al-Din Rumi (HarperOne, 2004)

The God of Small Things by Arundhati Roy (Random House, 1997)

The Hate U Give by Angie Thomas (Balzer + Bray, 2022)

The Insulted and Injured by Fyodor Dostoevsky (Wm. B. Eerdmans Publishing Co, 2011)

The Path Made Clear by Oprah Winfrey (Flatiron Books, 2019)

The Prince and the Pauper by Jaachynma N. E. Agu (Seaburn, 2009)

The Shade of My Own Tree by Sheila Williams (One World/Ballantine, 2003)

The Wonderful Wizard of Oz by Frank L. Baum (Penguin, 1995)

The World According to Mister Rogers: Important Things to Remember by Fred Rogers (Hyperion, 2003)

To Kill a Mockingbird by Harper Lee (Harper Perennial, 2002)

Travels with Myself and Another: A Memoir by Martha Gellhorn (TarcherPerigee, 2001)

Untamed by Glennon Doyle (The Dial Press, 2020)

Why Not Me? by Mindy Kaling (Three Rivers Press, 2016)

Winter of Artifice by Anaïs Nin (Obelisk Press, 1939)

You Learn by Living by Eleanor Roosevelt (John Knox Press, 1960)

ACKNOWLEDGMENTS

My deepest gratitude to my family and friends, who made writing this book during an especially overwhelming year possible; to Marian and Laurie, who have encouraged me every step of the way; and to Trevor and Nadi, who always, tirelessly, encourage me to be more confident in who I am.

ABOUT MEERA LEE PATEL

Meera Lee Patel is the self-taught artist and bestselling author of several books on mental and emotional health, including *Start Where You Are: A Journal for Self-Exploration* and *How It Feels to Find Yourself: Navigating Life's Changes with Purpose, Clarity, and Heart.* Her books and journals have sold over a million copies worldwide and have been translated into more than a dozen languages.

She lives with her family in St. Louis, Missouri. For more about Meera and her work, please visit meeralee.com or find her online @MeeraLeePatel.

ALSO BY

Meera Lee Patel

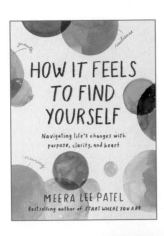

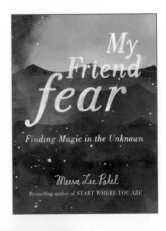

MEERALEE.COM